New Idiom A Day

A Day

Vol 1

INTRODUCTION:
Learning a new idiom a day is a great way to stimulate your mind.

ISBN-13: 978-1499697605
ISBN-10: 1499697600

Subscribe to New Idiom a Day

FeedBack@NewWordADay.com

On the back burner

The back burner refers to the back burner on a stove.

A burner is where the flame comes out on top of the oven.

Of course... the flame cooks the food.

The back burner on a stove is smaller than the front burners.

So... food cooks slower on the back burner.

It will take more time to cook.

It will take longer.

On the back burner = Let's slow it down

Let's use it

Ok. We can't agree on a color. Let's put it on the back burner.
Ok. We can't agree on a color. Let's get back to choosing a color later.
Ok. We can't agree on a color. Let's put other choices first before the color.

"On the back burner" = Let's decide later
"On the back burner" = Put the choice aside
"On the back burner" = Let's think about it later

Skate on thin ice

Skate refers to ice skating.

If we skate on thin ice... the ice might break and we can fall into the water.

So... when you skate on thin ice... you are in danger.

Let's us it....

You should talk nicer to him. You are skating on thin ice. You should talk nicer to him. You might get in trouble if you make him mad.

You kids are skating on thin ice when you tease the dog. You kids might get bit when you tease the dog.

Skate on thin ice = you are in danger

Tighten your belt

"You tighten your belt when you eat less."

Your belt around your belly can get smaller when you buy less food.

When you eat less... you spend less money.

So...

Tighten your belt = Spend less money

Let's use it...

I want to buy a bike so I will tighten my belt.
I want to buy a bike so I will save my money.

Tighten your belt = "Saving money"

Tighten your belt = Spending less money

I want to save money so I will tighten my belt.
I want to save money so I will spend less.

Tighten your belt = buy less stuff

Get out of Dodge

Dodge refers to a famous city from the old west.

Dodge was a wild city.

Dodge was a lawless city with mean outlaws.

So...

A mean cowboy would say... you better get out of Dodge!

Or...

A meek cowboy would say... I better get out of Dodge!

It was like saying...

This town is not big enough for the two of us. You better get out of Dodge!

Get out of Dodge = you better get out of here
Get out of Dodge = we should leave
Get out of Dodge = I should go

Let's use it

Uh oh! We broke the vase. We better get out of Dodge!
Uh oh! We broke the vase. We better run!

Here comes the boss. We better get out of dodge.
Here comes the boss. Let's get out of here.

Get out of Dodge = Run!

Fresh as a daisy

A daisy is a bright yellow flower with bright white pedals.
A daisy has a fresh scent.

Fresh means it smells nice and clean.
It is a very good smell.

When you think of a daisy- think fresh, new and bright.

So...

Fresh as a daisy means clean and new.

So...

Let's use it...

I ran for miles but I feel fresh as a daisy.
I ran for miles but I feel like I just started.

The shower made me fresh as a daisy because the water felt good.
The shower made me feel new and clean because the water felt good.

Am I tired? No. I feel fresh as a daisy.
Am I tired? No. I feel great.

Fresh as a daisy = I feel clean
Fresh as a daisy = I feel refreshed
Fresh as a daisy = I feel ready to go again
Fresh as a daisy = I have a lot of energy
Fresh as a daisy = I feel great

The Jury is still out.

Juries make decisions in a trial.

A jury decides guilt or innocence in a court of law.

When the jury is out... it is deciding the verdict.

It is deciding the guilt or innocence of a person.

The jury goes into a room and talks about the trial.

This is called being out.

A jury is made of people.

So... the people are deciding.

Let's use it...

You made a good sales presentation, but the jury is still out.
You made a good sales presentation, but they are still
deciding if they want to buy it.

I think we will move to a new house, but the jury is still out.
I think we will move to a new house, but have not decided
yet.

The Jury is still out = they are thinking about it

The Jury is still out = they have not made a decision yet

The Jury is still out = they will give an answer soon.

Mover and shaker

Used as...
They are the movers and shakers.

A mover and shaker refers to earthquakes.

During an earthquake... the ground moves.

The ground moves from side to side.

During an earthquake... everything shakes.

Trees shake, houses shake, everything shakes.

So...

Earthquakes are powerful.

Anything that can move and shake is very powerful.

So...
Let's use it....
He is a mover and shaker. He makes all the decisions.
He has the authority. He makes all the decisions.

She is a mover and shaker. She can say yes and buy your product.
She can spend money for the company. She can say yes and buy your product.

Mover and shaker = they are the boss
Mover and shaker =they have the power
Mover and shaker = they can get it done

"Don't count your chickens before they hatch"

Pretend you are a chicken farmer...

You have chicken eggs and you want to count the chicks in the eggs because you want to sell them.

You can't count the chickens in the eggs because some will not hatch.

So... if you only count eggs... you will think you can count on selling more chickens...
... than will come out of the eggs.

So... this means...

Don't count something that may not happen.

"Don't count your chickens before they hatch" = don't rely on something that has not happened yet
Let's use it...

I know you are going to sell your house, but don't count your chickens before they hatch.
I know you are going to sell your house, but it might not sell.

I know you got the job, but don't count your chickens before they hatch.
I know you got the job, but it's not real until your first day.

Don't count your chickens before they hatch = don't count on it

"Don't count your chickens before they hatch" = it may not happen

"A stitch in time saves nine"

You have a small tear in your shirt.

If you put a stitch in it... the tear will not get bigger...

... and you will not need to add more stitches.

Of course... a stitch is a small piece of thread used in sewing to join two pieces of clothing together.

You use a needle and thread and make a stitch.

If a rip starts to happen in your shirt... and you do not add a stitch to hold it... the rip will get bigger.

So one stitch saved you from having to put more in.

A stitch in time saves nine = If you do something early about it... it will not get worse.

Let's use it.

Your roof has a leak. You do nothing about it. It will get worse.

So... I can say to you...

I see you have a bad tile on your roof. A stitch in time saves nine.
I see you have a bad tile on your roof. You should fix it fast or water will come in and ruin the whole roof.

A stitch in time saves nine = Fix it now or it will be ruined later.

Don't give up your day job

Usually this phrase talks about something that is a hobby.

A hobby is something you do for fun but you make no money at it.

For example...

You paint art but no one pays you.

You write books but never publish them.

You make songs but never sing them for money.

You work at something for fun.

Ok...

So you show your hobby to someone else...

You show me the painted you painted.

You: What do you think of my painting?
ME: Don't give up your day job
YOU: Why do you say that?
Me: It's not good art. No one will ever buy it.

Don't give up your day job = It's not good enough to make money

Don't give up your day job = Don't try to replace your job with this hobby

Don't give up your day job = You won't make money so you will need to keep working

Me: How did you like the book I wrote?
You: Don't give up your day job. I did not like it.

Me: How did you like the book I wrote?
You: It was bad and it will never sell. I did not like it.

Don't give up your day job = I don't like it

Goes in one ear and out the other

If something goes in one ear and out the other...
... then it does not stay in your head.

If something does not stay in your head...
... you will quickly forget it.

This phrase always references spoken words.

Let's use it...

I give you advice, but it goes in one ear and out the other.
I give you advice, but you don't listen to me,
I give you advice, but you don't remember it.

Everything I say goes in one ear and out the other. I feel I am
talking to myself.
You ignore everything I say. I feel I am talking to myself.

"Goes in one ear and out the other" = you never listen

An eager beaver

Eager beaver describes the actions of a person.
Eager means to be enthusiastic and willing.
Eager means to be happy to do something.

A beaver is an animal.

A beaver builds dams and creates a lake so it can farm fish.

Beavers are famous for working hard.

So...

Eager beaver = Always ready to work hard

Eager beaver = A person who is happy to work hard

Let's use it...

We'll get Bill to work with us because he is an eager beaver.
We'll get Bill to work with us because he is a ready to please
and he is hard working.

I am an eager beaver. You can count on me.
I am happy to work hard. You can count on me.

Eager beaver is a compliment

Eager beaver = happy to work hard

All bark and no bite

A dog that barks does not always bite.

Just because a dog is barking... it does not mean it wants to hurt you.

Some dogs bark, but never bite.

So...

The dog is loud and scary but harmless.

Just like a person could be...

All bark and no bite = Makes a lot of noise but does nothing else

Let's use it...

Don't let the boss scare you. He is all bark and no bite.
Don't let the boss scare you. He yells a lot but that's all he will do.

Don't worry about his mean words. He is all bark and no bite.
Don't worry about his mean words. He acts mean but is actually nice.

All bark and no bite = don't get upset

Burn the midnight oil

People used to burn oil in lamps to light up their house at night.

So... if you wanted to read at night... you had to burn an oil lamp because light bulbs did not exist yet.

If you read late into the night... you will reach midnight.

Thus... you burned the midnight oil when you studied at midnight by an oil lamp.

Let's use it...

I will get the project done. I will burn the midnight oil.
I will get the project done. I will work all night.

I will pass the test tomorrow. I will burn the midnight oil.
I will pass the test tomorrow. I will study late into the night.

Burn the midnight oil = Work until late

Burn the midnight oil = Study into the night

"Don't put all your eggs in one basket"

Eggs in this case... means something of great value.
Eggs could mean businesses that you own.
Eggs could be stocks you own.

Eggs in this sentence usually means - something precious and fragile.

For example... the egg could mean money or jewelry.

The basket means one place.
The basket means a location where the valuables are kept.

Let's use it.
I only own airline stocks. I put all my eggs in one basket, but I watch the basket well.
I only own airline stocks. It is the only stock I own, but I watch the stocks for changes.

I own many different kinds of businesses. I don't put my eggs in one basket.
I own many different kinds of businesses. I am spread out for safety and one bad business will not put me out of business.

Don't put all your eggs in one basket. I keep my money in many places in my house.
Don't put your money in one spot. If someone steals it... it will all be gone. Make them look for it.

Don't put all your eggs in one basket = don't put a valuable in one spot. Put them in many spots to be safe.

Don't put all your eggs in one basket = Diversify

Nailing jelly to the wall

You cannot nail jelly to a wall.

Jelly is jam as in - peanut butter and jam.

You cannot use a hammer and nail to connect jam to the wall.

This is impossible.

So...

Nailing jelly to the wall = It is impossible to do

Nailing jelly to the wall = It cannot be done.

Let's use it.

Getting the contract signed is like nailing jelly to the wall.
Getting the contract signed is impossible.

Getting the cat to take a bath is like nailing jelly to the wall.
Getting the cat to take a bath is never going to happen.

Nailing jelly to the wall = It is not doable

Scrape the bottom of the barrel

Barrels were used to hold almost everything in the past.

So... when you got to the bottom of the barrel... whatever is in the barrel is almost gone.

The barrel is almost empty.

If you have to scrape the bottom of the barrel... then there is almost nothing left.

So...

Scrape the bottom of the barrel = there is nothing left

Let's use it.

I have one pen left that works. I am scraping the bottom of the barrel.
I have one pen left that works. There are almost no pens left.

I worked all night to come up with a story. I was scraping the bottom of the barrel.
I worked all night to come up with a story. I came up with almost no stories.

Scrape the bottom of the barrel = There is almost nothing left

No use crying over spilled milk

Milk was very rare and valuable a long time ago.

So if you spilled it... it was quite a loss.

If you spill milk... you cannot drink it...

... so it is lost.

If the milk is spilled.... you cannot put it back in the bowl.

There is nothing you can do to get the milk back in the bowl.

You lost something valuable and there's nothing you can do about it.

Let's use it.

You lost a lot of money. There's no use crying over spilt milk. You lost a lot of money. Forget about it because it is gone and there is nothing you can do about it.

No use crying over spilled milk = No use crying about bad things that happened

No use crying over spilled milk = Forget it and move on

A penny for your thoughts

A penny bought a lot in the past.

For example: One hundred years ago... you could buy an apple with a penny.

So...

... a penny had value.

If I offer something of value for your thoughts...

... I am saying your thoughts are worth a lot.

So...

A penny for your thoughts = what you think is valuable to me

Let's use it.

You look worried. "A penny for your thoughts?"
You look worried. What you are worried about is important to me.

I need to decide what to do. "A penny for your thoughts?"
I need to decide what to do. What you think will help me decide.

A penny for your thoughts = Tell me what you think

"Cut to the chase"

The chase is the most exciting part of a movie.

The movie is boring to watch compared to the chase.

The chase refers to any kind of chase.

For example...

A car chase... a chase with horses... a foot chase.

The bad guy is chasing the good guy...

or...

The good guy is chasing the bad guy.

The rest of the movie is boring compared to the chase scene.

The chase is the interesting point in the movie.

So...
Cut to the chase = Get to the point
Cut to the chase = Get to the interesting part
Cut to the chase = Please talk about the exciting part

Let's use it.

I think your product is interesting. Let's cut to the chase. How much does it cost?
I think your product is interesting. Let's get to the important part. How much does it cost?

Cut to the chase = talk about the most important thing.

"Actions speak louder than words"

The "actions" refers to what a person does.
The words are what a person says.

A person can tell you something.
A person can do something other than what they say.

For example:
A person says: I never eat junk food.

Then...
You always see them eating junk food.

So you say:
I know you say you don't eat bad food, but actions speak louder than words.
I know you say you don't eat bad food, but you are always eating junk food.

Actions speak louder than words = you say one thing and do another

Actions speak louder than words = what you do does not match what you said you would do.

Let's use it again...

You said I could trust you, but actions speak louder than words because I caught you stealing.
You said I could trust you, but you lied because I caught you stealing.

Actions speak louder than words = you lied about your intentions.

The ball is in your court

This refers to tennis.

The ball is in your court when I hit it back to you with my tennis racket.

It is now on your side of the court and it is your turn to hit it back.

There is nothing I can do, but watch you hit the ball.

So...

The ball is in your court = it is your turn

Let's use it.

I finished my part of the report. The ball is in your court.
I finished my part of the report. It's your turn to work on it.

I sent the contract to them. The ball is in their court.
I sent the contract to them. We are waiting for them to sign it.

The ball is in your court = I must wait for you to act now

A picture paints a thousand words

You can write words to describe something.

Or...

You can draw a picture.

It would take many words to tell what you could just show with a picture.

A picture tells you many different things.

For example:

You draw a dog.

You can see what kind of dog it is.
You can see what color it is.
You can see how big the dog is.

You can see many things quickly that would take many words to explain.

So...

A picture paints a thousand words = It's quicker to show you.

Let's use it.

I can give you the instructions, but a picture paints a thousand words. Let me get you the blueprints.
I can give you the instructions, but it will be easier if you see how it is done. Let me get you the blueprints.

Everything but the kitchen sink

The kitchen sink is connected to the wall

If you took everything from a house...
.... and put it into a truck...

... only the kitchen sink would be left.

So... it is a funny way of saying "everything"

What is in the bag? "Everything but the kitchen sink."
What is in the bag? "Too many items to list."

Your room is filled with everything but the kitchen sink.
Your room is filled with a lot of stuff.

Everything but the kitchen sink = A lot of stuff
"Everything but the kitchen sink" = everything we could
think of

"Everything but the kitchen sink" = tons of items

"A horse of a different color "

You see a nice brown horse in my yard.

You describe it to me and say you want to buy it.

You say it had a pink bow on its tail.

I realize you're talking about the black horse because only the black horse has a bow.

I tell you: That's a horse of a different color.

A horse of a different color = you are talking about the wrong thing

A horse of a different color = you are speaking about something else

Let's use it....

You: I saw a man on a thing with two wheels and a motor. I think it was a bicycle.

Me: No. You're thinking of a motorcycle. That's a horse of a different color.
Me: No. You're thinking of a motorcycle. That's not a bike, but it's like one.
Me: No. You're thinking of a motorcycle. That's not a bike, but it is similar.

Can't make heads or tails of it

You see an animal in the bushes.

You can't tell if you are looking at the head...
You can't tell if you are looking at the tail...
...because the leaves are in the way.

So...

You don't know what animal you are looking at.

You can't see enough of it.

You don't understand what it is.

So...

Can't make heads or tails of it = I don't see it
"Can't make heads or tails of it" = I don't understand it

Let's use it.

I can't make heads or tails of it. You'll have to rewrite it.
I can't read this. You'll have to rewrite it.

Math is confusing to me. I can't make heads or tails of it.
Math is confusing to me. I can't figure it out.

Can't make heads or tails of it = I am confused

Beat around the bush

A bird hides in the bush.
You want to capture the bird.
So... you beat the bush to flush out the bird.
The goal is to make the bird come out by scaring it.

So...
If you beat around the bush... the bird will never come out.
If you beat around the bush... you are not beating the bush...
... and the bird will not be chased out into the open.

You are not making the bird come out... you are failing to
make it happen.
You are avoiding what needs to be done to meet your goal.

Beat around the bush = never getting something done
Beat around the bush = not getting something done that you
could easily do

Let's use it...
You could tell me where the treasure is buried, but you are
beating around the bush.
You could tell me where the treasure is buried, but you are
changing the topic.

Don't beat around the bush. Give me an answer.
Don't evade my question with small talk. Give me an answer.

Me: Did you eat the last cookie?
You: Cookies are not good for you.
Me: I'll ask again. Did you eat the last cookie?
You: What cookies?
Me: Stop beating around the bush and answer me!

Beat around the bush = Avoid doing something you could do

All in the same boat

Used as...
If you are in the same boat as me... then you have to go where I go.

It also implies that we do not control the boat.

It means that we are in the same situation.
Or...
We are in the same predicament.

We are on the same journey that we do no control.

All in the same boat usually means that we both cannot do anything about it.
We are stuck in the same boat.

So...
We are all in the same boat.
We are all in the same boat so we should work together.
We are all in the same boat so we should work together to find our way back.

Me: I can't believe the teacher gave us eight hours of homework!
You: We are all in the same boat so let's do the homework together.

"We are all in the same boat" = I am trapped too
"We are all in the same boat" = I have to do it too
"We are all in the same boat" = it is the same for me

Monkey Business

A monkey would not understand business.
A monkey would act silly instead of doing business because it is not smart.
So... monkey business is the opposite of the business that should be done.
For example...
Business executives are sitting in an office.
They should be working on a report.
Instead... they are throwing things at each other.
They are doing monkey business instead of working.
They hear someone coming.
One of them says: Hey! Stop the monkey business! Someone is coming!
They are playing around when they should be working.
They are doing what monkeys would do if they were in the room.
Monkeys would not do any work.
They would throw things and play.
So... monkey business means to be doing something that you should not do.
It can mean you are doing something very bad as well.
Such as...
Hey! I see you stealing money! Stop the monkey business!

So...
Monkey business = Doing something wrong

He started the monkey business when I left the room.
He started the monkey business as soon as I left the room.
The children started misbehaving as soon as I left the room.

Monkey business = Playing when you should be serious

Monkey business = Being out of control

Stick out your Neck

Think of a goose.

It is risky for a goose to stick out its neck.

A goose is very helpless when it extends its neck.

It exposes its neck to danger.

Just like the goose...
...You are taking a risk when you stick out your neck.

You neck is open for attack when you lift your chin...
... your neck is now sticking out.

So...
Let's use it.

You are sticking your neck out by giving him money.
You risk losing money by giving him money.

I was sticking my neck when I gave a stranger a car ride.
I could have gotten hurt when I gave a stranger a ride.

I am sticking my neck out by trusting him
I could get into trouble by trusting him.

I will stick my neck out and help you.
I will put myself in danger and help you.

Sticking your neck out = you are taking a big risk

See through rose-colored glasses

Eyeglasses are made of clear glass.

You see right through them.

Rose-colored eyeglasses are made of pink colors.

Things look pink when you look through them.

So... a white wall will look pretty and pink.

The wall will look better than it really is.

Everything will look prettier because of the rose color.

All will look better.

So...

Let's use it.

He is never sad because he sees through rose-colored glasses.
He is never sad because he sees things better than they are.

She is always happy because she sees the world through rose-colored glasses.
She is always happy because she sees the world as a good place.

See through rose-colored glasses = See things better than they are

Scratch my back and I'll scratch yours

We cannot scratch our own back.

So...

... we need someone else to scratch our back.

You help someone when you scratch his or her back.

So... we help each other.

So...

... let's use it...

I will give you the money. Scratch my back and I'll scratch yours. Get me tickets to the game.
I will give you the money. I'll help you if you help me. Get me tickets to the game.

Scratch my back and I'll scratch yours = I will help you if you help me.

A bird in the hand is worth two in the bush

You are a bird lover.
You caught a bird in your hand.
You see two in the bushes.

If you try to capture the birds in the bushes...
... you will probably drop the bird you have.

The bird in the bushes will fly away...
... and the bird you dropped will fly away too.

So...
If you chase two birds in the bush...
... you will end up with no birds.

You should not chase something that you may not get when
you have something for sure.
Or...
You should not do something risky when you have something
safe.

Let's use it.
You have a great job. A bird in the hand is worth two in the
bush. Don't quit.
You have a great job. Your new job might not be as good.
Don't quit.

So... the idea is...
Do not chase the unknown when you know something is
good.

A bird in the hand is worth two in the bush = Keep what you
know is good and don't risk it for
something that may or may not be good.

Keep your fingers crossed

People put their middle finger over their index finger because they think it will bring them luck.

That is called crossing your fingers.

They hold their hand up with the two fingers over and under...
... and at the same time they say: Wish me luck.

Crossing your fingers is a superstition that people believe will bring them luck.

So...

When someone says: Cross your fingers.

It means... Let's hope for luck.

Keep your fingers crossed = Let's hope for the best

Let's use it.

A storm is coming. Keep your fingers crossed that we are okay.
A storm is coming. Let's hope for luck and that we are okay.

Keep your fingers crossed = Keep hoping for luck

A drop in the bucket

The bucket has water in it.

Add one drop of water and you see no change because the drop is lost in all the water.

Adding one drop of water makes no difference.

One new drop has no effect on the water in the bucket.

So...

A drop in the bucket = You can't see a difference

A drop in the bucket = It appears to have no effect

I gave money to feed cats, but it's just a drop in the bucket because there are so many
hungry cats,

I gave money to feed cats, but it has no effect because there are so many hungry cats.

I gave money to feed cats, but it will help little because there are so many hungry cats.

A drop in the bucket = It will barely help

Get cracking

Get cracking means to get going.

Get on it.

Go.

Start.

Here are the tools you need. Get cracking.
Here are the tools you need. Start the project.

Here is the paintbrush. Get cracking.
Here is the paintbrush. Start Painting.

Get cracking = Get started

Rub the wrong way

He rubs the wrong way.

You rub me the wrong way.

Rub means to touch someone or something by moving and pressing your fingers.

You rub the hair of a cat when you pet it.

You can rub your hair the wrong way.

Your hair will stand up If you rub it the wrong way

You get angry because your hair is annoying when it sticks up.

Your hair will bother you.

So...

Bill rubs me the wrong way because he always insults me.

Bill annoys me because he always insults me.

Sally rubs me the wrong way because her voice is annoying.

Sally bothers me because he voice is annoying.

Rub the wrong way = to annoy

Rub the wrong way = to bother

Suffer fools gladly

Often used as... He does not suffer fools gladly.

When we suffer a fool ...
...it means that we are interacting with a foolish person
... and their foolishness is bothering us

Their foolishness is making us suffer
They are a fool and a fool makes mistakes

A fool is dumb and it usually means we are dealing with a
dumb person

Dealing with a fool means we are... working with a fool
or
we are partners with a fool

You have a co-worker who is always wrong and you have to
fix his mistakes
or
You have a partner who always has bad ideas because he is a
fool

Suffer gladly means that you are happy to continue to interact
with this fool

Suffer gladly means you don't leave and you continue to work
with the fool

He does not suffer fools gladly. He will argue with them.
He does not accept stupid ideas. He will argue with them.

He does not suffer fools gladly and he got another job.
He does not want to work with idiots and he got another job.
Suffer fools gladly = Ignore the actions of a stupid person

Between a rock and a hard place

A rock sits on hard ground...
... the hard ground is the hard place

Anything between a rock and a hard place cannot move

It has no place to go and is stuck there

So... if someone or something is between a rock and a hard place...

... it or they are stuck there.

It means you have nothing good to do.
You have no good move to make.

You will lose no matter what move you make because you are between a rock and a hard place.
You will lose no matter what move you make because you do not have good move to make.

If we sell the business we will lose money, but we can't afford to keep it. We are between a
rock and a hard place because we will lose some money no matter what we decide to do.

Between a rock and a hard place = There is nothing good to do
Between a rock and a hard place = There is no good move to make

Between a rock and a hard place = It is bad no matter what we decide to do

Between a rock and a hard place = We have no good options

When it rains it pours

Think of pour as in to pour a drink.
Or…
"To pour a glass of juice."

A lot comes out when you pour a liquid.

So when it rains… it does not rain a little… as far as you are concerned because even a little rain gets you wet.

Once it starts raining, you can count on it to rain a lot more.

Now…
Let's use it.

My books are selling very well. When it rains, it pours.

My books are selling very well. Once the books start selling, the sales really grow.

People found out I sell the best cake. When it rains, it pours.

People found out I sell the best cake. Once one person came everyone came.

When it rains, it pours = Once something happens, it happens a lot more

When it rains, it pours = Once something bad starts, it will get worse

When it rains, it pours = Once something good starts, it will get even better

When it rains, it pours = Once it starts, there is no stopping it

Piece of cake

A piece of cake is easy to eat.

So... it is something that is easy to do.

We say something is a piece of cake when it is easy to do as well.

So...

I passed my test. It was a piece of cake.

I passed my test. It was easy to do.

Me: Wow. You did that fast.
You: Piece of cake.

Piece of cake = Easy to do

You can't judge a book by its cover

You can't tell how good a book will be by looking at how good the cover is

A book can have a good cover and it can be a bad book

A book can have a bad cover and be a great read.

The same goes for anything.

You can't judge anything by the way it looks.

A car can look slow, but it can be very fast.

Someone can look unintelligent and yet turn out to be a genius.

A person can look weak and turn out in fact to be very strong.

So...

I thought he was mean, but you can't judge a book by its cover. He turned out to be very nice.

The business looked like it would fail, but it was very good. You can't judge a book by its cover.

You can't judge a book by its cover = You can tell how good it is by the way it looks

Go down like a lead balloon

A balloon floats up into the air.

A balloon made out of lead would quickly fall.

We expect a balloon to float up.

The balloon is like an idea that we have.

Floating up means to be successful.

We expect our idea to be successful.

We are surprised when we release the balloon and it falls because it's made of lead.

Lead is a heavy metal.

We are surprised when we do something and it fails...
... but we expected it to succeed.

Go down like a lead balloon = my idea unexpectedly failed
Go down like a lead balloon = It failed
Go down like a lead balloon = No one liked it

I thought it was a good idea, but I soon found it would go down like a lead balloon.

I thought it was a good idea, but it turned out to be a bad idea.

I presented my idea, but it went down like a lead balloon.

I presented my idea, but no one liked it.

The early bird catches the worm

Early means: To get out of bed early in the morning.

Early means: To wake up before others.

You get there before the others when you wake up early.

The bird catches the worm and gets a meal.

The bird gets something accomplished.

The bird achieves something good.

Wake up early and get good things because you get there before other people.

You: I found a good job because I was the first one there.
Me: Yes. The early bird gets the worm.

"Once in a blue moon"

A blue moon is very rare.

You can see a blue moon in the sky about once a year.

So... it is rare.

"Once in a blue moon" = "It will not happen often"

"Once in a blue moon" = "It will be rare"

"Once in a blue moon" = "It occurs once in a while."

I don't own an umbrella because it only rains once in a blue moon."

I don't own an umbrella because it barely ever rains "

An albino lion is born once in a blue moon.

An albino lion is born on rare occasions.

Once in a blue moon = it happens seldom

Once in a blue moon = it hardly ever happens

Pulling my leg

It means to trick someone by telling them a lie.

You are pulling my leg.

It comes from...

A crook in London would tackle his victim and rob them.

They would pull them to the ground by the leg and steal their money.

It often means that the person is teasing you in a friendly way.

There's a diamond in the box? Oh come on. You are pulling me leg.

There's a diamond in the box? Oh come on. You are kidding me.

There's a diamond in the box? Oh come on. You are tricking me.

I don't know if she is pulling my leg or not.

I wonder if she is pulling my leg.

It does not mean that your leg is actually pulled.

"You are pulling my leg" = "You are lying to me"

It takes two to tango

A tango is a dance where the dancers stay close and hold hands.

So... the dance needs two dancers.

You cannot dance the tango alone.

It is something that takes two people to do.

So... think of something that takes two people to do.

Such as...

It takes two people to fight.

Let's use it...

He may have started the fight, but it takes two to tango.

He may have started the fight, but you were fighting too.

"It takes two to tango" = "You are doing it too"

Don't make a mountain out of a molehill

A mole is a furry little animal.

They live in a hole in a little mound called a molehill.

A mound is a little hill.

A molehill is little.

A mountain is big.

Don't make a mountain out of a molehill.
Don't make something big out of something small.

Usually...

Don't make it into a big problem and worry because it is only a little problem.

So...

Okay. You had a little argument with him. Don't make a mountain out of a molehill.

Okay. You had a little argument with him. Don't make it into a big issue.

"Don't make a mountain out of a molehill" = "Don't let a little problem worry you."

Don't look a gift horse in the mouth

You look into the mouth of a horse to see if it is healthy.

You check the mouth of a horse before you buy it because you want to know you are buying a good horse.

So... if someone gives you a horse for free... you should just accept it because it is rude to be ungrateful.

It is rude to complain about a gift that someone gives you.

For example:

I give you a free car and you complain about the color? Don't look a gift horse in the mouth!

"Don't look a gift horse in the mouth" = "Don't complain about the small details of a free gift"

Walk on eggshells

You have to walk gently on eggshells to avoid breaking them.

So... you have to be very careful and it is very hard not to break them.

Walk on eggshells is usually said as...

You have to walk on eggshells when you are around him because he is easily insulted.

You have to be very careful about what you say because he is easily insulted.

"Walk on eggshells " = "You have to be careful"

Cross your fingers

Comes from: People cross their index and middle finger as a superstition that doing so will bring them luck.

You cross your fingers by putting one finger under the other on the same hand.

A superstition is a belief that doing something can affect something else by magic.
Touching your nose to bring you luck for example.

Hope for the best.

Hope to be lucky.

Cross your fingers and hope we arrive safely.

Cross your fingers = Hope to get lucky

Big fish in a small pond

Comes from: The idea that a big fish in a small pond will have an easy life by being in charge of the little fishes.

The big fish has no competition.

The main idea is:
Someone is successful only because he has no competition.

If the big fish were in the big pond - things would be difficult.

So...

He is a big fish in a small pond. That is the only reason he wins so easily.

It is a way to say he only wins because he has no competition.

He is a big league player and plays in the small leagues.

It is meant to say:
He would not do so well if he had real challengers.

Big fish in a small pond = He is not that good.

Spill the beans

Comes from: You let the beans out of the can when spill them.

You can't count beans when they're in a can.
They can be counted when you spill them out of the can.

So... now the number of beans is known.

The number of beans is no longer a secret.

So...

The secret is out.

I will spill the beans and tell everyone your secret.

Spill the beans = I will tell your secret

The cat is out of the bag

You don't know what is in the bag.

Everyone knows a cat is in the bag after the bag is opened.

So... the secret of what is in the bag is now known.

The secret is out.

She knew I had the letter when it fell out of my pocket. The cat is out of the bag.

She now knows I secretly had the letter.

It is impossible to get a cat back into a bag once it gets out.

So it is a secret that cannot be forgotten once known.

The secret is out.

Back to the drawing board

A drawing board is used to design things.

It is used to draw plans.

So... we have to go back to the drawing board to redo our plan or design.

We have to redo our plan because the current plan is not working.

That's is an unexpected bug. I guess it's back to the drawing board and I will have to rewrite the program.

The plan has to be redone.

When pigs fly

Pigs cannot fly.

A pig will never fly.

So it is impossible.

Or...

When the impossible happens.

I will give you the money when pigs fly.

I will give you the money when something impossible happens.

Meaning... I will never give you the money. Ever

I will never do that.

Cat got your tongue?

Cat got your tongue? Why don't you answer?

Do you not want to answer the question?
Are you are so surprised that you cannot speak?
Do you have nothing to say?

You cannot answer since a cat took your tongue.

This is often because you are shocked and cannot think of something to say.

It often means that you can answer, but do not want to because it would admit guilt.

Barking up the wrong tree.

That is wrong. You are barking up the wrong tree.

We are looking for something in the wrong place.
The idea I have about something is wrong.
You are mistaken.

A dog barks up the wrong tree when he thinks the animal he
is chasing is up in a tree.
The animal is not and so the dog is wrong.

Put it together for fun...

Detective speaking to the suspect:
Did you steal the money? Cat got your tongue?
Okay. Don't answer me.
I know you have a history of stealing and a leopard can't
change his spots.
So... you must have done it.
Or tell me. Am I barking up the wrong tree?

A Leopard can't change his spots.

He says he will become honest, but a Leopard can't change his spots.

You cannot change who you are.
He can never change the way he acts.
You cannot change something you were born with.

You cannot change something about you that is out of your control.

This often means you cannot change a trait that you are born with.
You are born dishonest and will never change because this saying implies such things are unchangeable.